Animal World

LIVE. LEARN. DISCOVER.

Acknowledgments

All artwork supplied by Myke Taylor, The Art Agency

Photo credits:
b—bottom, t—top, r—right, l—left, m—middle

Cover: t Corbis/Karine Aigner, b Corbis/Frans Lanting, bl Corbis/Sea World of California, bm Corbis/DLILLC, br Corbis/DLILLC

Poster: dreamstime.com/Anthony Hathaway

1 Dreamstime.com/David Davis, 2-3 Corbis/Kennan Ward, 4tl Dreamstime.com/Kiyoshi Takahase Segundo, 4tr Dreamstime.com/Fred Goldstein, 4ml Dreamstime.com/Carolyne Pehora, 4-5m Digital Vision, 5b Dreamstime.com/Wei Send Chen, 6-7 Corbis/Kevin Schafer, 8 Dreamstime.com/Anthony Hathaway, 9t all Dreamstime.com, 9b Dreamstime.com, 10t Dreamstime.com/Robert Gubiani, 10b Dreamstime.com/Dennis Sabo, 11t Dreamstime.com/Cathy Figuli, 11m Dreamstime.com, 11b Dreamstime.com/Asther Lau Choon Siew, 12t Dreamstime.com/Dusty Cline, 14t Dreamstime.com/Carolina K. Smith m.d., 14b Dreamstime.com/Richard Gunion, 15t Dreamstime.com/Joao Estevao Andrade de Freitas, 15m Dreamstime.com/Paul Cowan, 15b Dreamstime.com/Marek Kosmal, 16t Dreamstime.com/Nico Smit, 16b Dreamstime.com, 17t Dreamstime.com/Simone van den Berg, 17b Dreamstime.com/Uzi Hen, 18t Dreamstime.com/Joao Estevao Andrade de Freitas, 19t Dreamstime.com/Wichittra Srisunon, 20t Dreamstime.com/Fulvio Evangelista, 20b Dreamstime.com/Dawn Allyn, 21t Dreamstime.com/Caroline Henri, 21b Dreamstime.com, 22t Dreamstime.com/Rayna Canedy, 22b Dreamstime.com/Asther Lau Choon Siew, 23t Dreamstime.com/Tom Davison, 23m Dreamstime.com/Asther Lau Choon Siew, 23b Dreamstime.com/Martina Misar, 24t Dreamstime.com/Asther Lau Choon Siew, 24b Dreamstime.com/Asther Lau Choon Siew, 25t Dreamstime.com/Robert Daniels, 25m Dreamstime.com/Kelly Bates, 25b Dreamstime.com/James Hearn, 26t Dreamstime.com/Ian Scott, 198b Dreamstime.com/Asther Lau Choon Siew, 27t Dreamstime.com/John Abramo, 27m Dreamstime.com/Johnny Lye, 27b Dreamstime.com/Asther Lau Choon Siew, 28t Dreamstime.com/Pamela Hodson, 28b Dreamstime.com/Feng Yu, 29t Dreamstime.com/Dallas Powell, jr., 29m Dreamstime.com/Heidi Hart, 29b Dreamstime.com/Tim Haynes, 30tl Dreamstime.com/Steffen Foerster, 30b Dreamstime.com/Holger Leyrer, 31t Dreamstime.com/Dmitrii Korovin, 31m Dreamstime.com/Anita Huszti, 31b Dreamstime.com/Lukáš Hejtman, 32tl Dreamstime.com/Hannu Liivaar, 32b Dreamstime.com/Paul Wolf, 33t Dreamstime.com/Darren Baker, 33m Dreamstime.com/Gert Very, 33b Dreamstime.com/Andy Heyward, 34t Dreamstime.com/Michael Johansson, 34b Dreamstime.com/Xavier Marchant, 35t Dreamstime.com/Laurin Rinder, 35m Dreamstime.com/Heather Craig, 35b Dreamstime.com, 36b Dreamstime.com, 37t Dreamstime.com/Roger Whiteway, 37m Dreamstime.com, 37b Dreamstime.com/Martina Berg, 39 Corbis/Steve Kaufman, 40 Digital Vision, 41tr Dreamstime.com/Willie Manalo, 41tl Digital Vision, 41br Dreamstime.com/Kiyoshi Takahase Segundo, 42tl Digital Vision, 42b Dreamstime.com/Ivan Chuyev, 43tl Dreamstime.com/Vaida Petreikiene, 43br Digital Vision, 44m Dreamstime.com/Scott Impink, 44bl Dreamstime.com/Johannes Gerhardus Swanepoel, 45tr Digital Vision, 45b Digital Vision, 46 Corbis, 47tr Dreamstime.com/Angela Farley, 47ml Dreamstime.com, 47bl Dreamstime.com/Paul Cowan, 48tr Digital Vision, 48b Dreamstime.com/Bobby Deal, 49tr Dreamstime.com/Fred Goldstein, 49br Dreamstime.com/Sanja Stepanovic, 51 Corbis/Kennan Ward, 52tl Dreamstime.com/Phil Date, 52br Dreamstime.com/Kathy Wynn, 53tr Dreamstime.com , 53m Tall Tree Ltd, 53b Dreamstime.com/Michael Ledray, 54tl Digital Vision, 54bl Digital Vision, 55t Dreamstime.com/Robert Hambley, 55b Dreamstime.com/Jorge Felix Costa, 56b Dreamstime.com/Tony Campbell, 57t Digital Vision, 57mr Dreamstime.com/Robert Hambley, 57br Dreamstime.com, 58–59 Dreamstime.com/Stefan Ekernas, 58bl Dreamstime.com, 59m Digital Vision, 59r Dreamstime.com, 60t Digital Vision, 60b Dreamstime.com/Joe Gough, 61t Dreamstime.com, 61b Dreamstime.com/Andreas Steinbach, 63 Corbis/Jeffrey L. Rotman, 64m Dreamstime.com/Ellen McIlroy, 65r Digital Vision, 65b Dreamstime.com, 66–67 Dreamstime.com/Matthias Weinrich, 66bl Dreamstime.com/Asther Lau Choon Siew, 66br Dreamstime.com/Asther Lau Choon Siew, 67t Dreamstime.com/Ian Scott, 67b Dreamstime.com/Asther Lau Choon Siew, 68t Dreamstime.com/Harald Bolten, 69 Dreamstime.com/Jeremy Bruskotter, 69m Dreamstime.com, 69b Dreamstime.com, 70t Dreamstime.com/Jeff Waibel, 70b Dreamstime.com, 71tr Dreamstime.com, 71br Dreamstime.com, 72t Dreamstime.com/Mike Brake, 72b Dreamstime.com/Michael L., 73t Dreamstime.com/Dallas Powell, jr., 73b Dreamstime.com/Holger Leyrer, 75 Tashka/Dreamstime.com, 76t Dreamstime.com/Anthony Hathaway, 76b Dreamstime.com/Steffen Foerster, 77t Dreamstime.com, 77b Dreamstime.com/Holger Wulschlaeger, 78tl Dreamstime.com/Steve Schowiak, 78b Dreamstime.com/Vladimir Pomortsev, 79t Dreamstime.com, 79b Digital Vision, 80 Dreamstime.com, 81br Corbis/DK Limited, 82 Dreamstime.com/Rick Parsons, 82tl Dreamstime.com/Keith Yong, 83tr Dreamstime.com/Kaleb Timberlake, 83br Dreamstime.com/Sascha Burkard, 84t Tall Tree Ltd, 84b Dreamstime.com/Nicola Gavin, 85t Dreamstime.com/Xavier Marchant, 85ml Dreamstime.com/Wael Hamdan, 85br Dreamstime.com/Piotr Bieniecki, 87 Dreamstime.com/Wang Sanjun, 88 Dreamstime.com/Fah mun Kwan, 89br Dreamstime.com/Nico Smit, 90tr Dreamstime.com/Steven Pike, 90b Dreamstime.com/Steffen Foerster, 91t Digital Vision, 91b Dreamstime.com/John Bloor, 92tr Dreamstime.com/Anthony Hathaway, 92bl Dreamstime.com/Jostein Hauge, 93t iStockphoto.com, 93br Dreamstime.com/Ethan Kocak

mountains 82-3

national parks 89, 90
nene 93
nematodes 13
nests 42-3, 44
newts 30, 72

oceans 64-71
orangutans 52
organic farming 91
ostriches 34, 45
owls 41

pandas 89
paradise flycatchers 42
parasites 12, 21
pelicans 35
pigeons 85
pigs 91
pikes 29
piranhas 28
platypuses 36
poison 18, 20, 26, 30, 31
poison arrow frogs 30
polar bears 8, 76
primates 37
puffins 77

rabbits 60, 61
racoons 85
rain forests 52-3
rats 37
rays 26, 65, 71
reptiles 8, 9, 32-3
rhinos 89
rodents 37
sailfish 64
salamanders 31

sand dollars 25
scorpions 20, 21, 79
sea cucumbers 24
sea dragons 27
sea otters 71
sea slugs 23
sea urchins 25
seals 76, 92
sharks 9, 26, 67, 68
shrews 37
shrimp 16
skeletons 9
snails 23
species 8
spiders 20-1, 81
sponges 10
starfish 24, 25
storks 43
sunstars 25
swallows 40, 41, 42
swans 35

takahe 93
tapeworms 12
ticks 20, 21
tigers 89
toads 31
tortoises 33
toucans 52
tuataras 33
tuna 64
turtles 32, 69

vertebrates 8

wasps 57
water fleas 17
weaver birds 43
whales 69
wild boar 55
wildebeest 59

wildfowl 35
wings 40, 41, 46, 47, 48
wood lice 17
worms 12-13
wrens 55

yaks 83

zebras 59

Index

alligators 32
amphibians 8, 30-1, 72
anemones 10
angelfish 27, 64
animal kingdom 8
anteaters 37
ants 15
apes and monkeys 37
arachnids 20-1
Arctic 76-7
arthropods 14

badgers 60
bats 46-7, 80
bighorn sheep 82
birds 8, 9, 34-5,
    40-45, 52, 53, 55,
    57, 77, 85, 89, 90, 93
bison 92
blue jays 57
blue tits 43
butterflies 14, 49

capybaras 37
carp 29
catfish 28
cave fish 81
caves 80-1
centipedes 18
chameleons 52, 53
cichlids 29, 73
cities 84-5
clams 22, 67
cockroaches 15
coral reefs 66-7
corals 11, 66
crabs 16

crocodiles 33, 59, 88
crustaceans 16-17
cuckoos 44
cuttlefish 22, 69

deer 56
deserts 78-9
dinosaurs 89
dodos 89
dragonflies 15, 48, 73
ducks 35

eagles 43, 45
echinoderms 24
eels 27
extinction 87, 88-9, 92

falcons 85
fish 8, 9, 26-9, 64-5,
    67, 68-9, 70, 71,
    73, 81
fleas 14, 17
forests 51-7
foxes 61, 77, 78, 84
frogs 30, 31

gannets 40
garibaldi fish 70
geckos 79
geese 35
golden lion tamarins
    93
gorillas 37
grasslands 58-61
gulls 35

habitat 51-61, 63-73, 75-85

habitat conservation
    90-1
herons 34
honeybees 49
houseflies 48
humans 37
hummingbirds 41, 42
hyenas 58

insects 7, 14-15, 48-9,
    53, 57, 73, 78
invertebrates 8, 10, 22

jellyfish 10, 11

kangaroos 36
katydids 53
kelp 70-1

ladybugs 49
lakes and ponds 72-3
limpets 23
llamas 61
lobsters 17
locusts 78
lynxes 57
macaws 53
mammals 8, 9, 36-7, 46
marmots 83
marsupials 36
meerkats 59
mice 37
millipedes 18, 19, 54
mites 20, 21
moles 37
mollusks 22-3
mountain goats 82, 83

The nene

The nene, or Hawaiian goose, is found only on the Hawaiian Islands. In 1949, there were fewer than 30 left. Some of these were caught and taken to breeding centers around the world. Now, more than 1,000 birds live in the wild.

Did you know? The takahe is a flightless bird that lives in New Zealand. People thought it was extinct in 1898, but it was rediscovered 50 years later.

Golden lion tamarins

By 1984, fewer than 100 golden lion tamarins survived in the forests of Brazil. Luckily, more of these monkeys have been bred in zoos and released back into the wild.

Saving our wildlife

Saved

Some animals have been saved from extinction. This has happened because people have stopped killing them and zoos have bred them to increase their numbers.

The European bison is related to the American buffalo.

Hunted

Northern fur seals were hunted for their fur and were almost extinct by the early 1900s. In 1911, the people killing the seals agreed to stop hunting them. Since then, the number of fur seals has increased.

European bison

Because of hunting, the European bison, or wisent, disappeared from the wild in 1927. But 50 bison still lived in zoos, and these produced young. Bison have now been released back into forests in Poland and Russia.

Cleaning up

Everybody can help to protect animal habitats. Garbage can be harmful to animals, so these people are clearing it from a pond.

Organic farming

Many farmers use chemicals called pesticides and fertilizers to grow their crops. These chemicals can harm wildlife. Chemicals are not used on an organic farm, so wild animals are not harmed.

These pigs on an organic farm are free range, which means they are allowed to walk outside.

Saving our wildlife

Conserving animals

The best way to save endangered animals is to conserve, or protect, their habitats. This can be done by creating national parks and by stopping farms and factories from polluting the land.

Watching animals

Some African countries, such as South Africa, have turned large areas into game reserves and national parks. Animals that live inside these areas are protected from human hunters.

Bird watching

People can watch animals in protected areas. This building is called a blind, and people use it to watch birds without disturbing them.

Many tourists visit game reserves and national parks to watch the animals.

Did you know? The world's first national park was the Yellowstone National Park. It was created in 1872.

Terrible lizards

Dinosaurs disappeared 65 million years ago. They may have become extinct because the world's climate changed.

Dinosaurs, such as *Tyrannosaurus rex*, might not have survived in the new climate.

Hunted to death

Dodos were a kind of flightless bird that lived on Mauritius in the Indian Ocean. They became extinct in the 1600s because they were hunted by humans.

Did you know?

In 2006, the World Conservation Union published a list of 16,119 animals, plants, and fungi that may become extinct.

Under threat

Many well-known animals could become extinct in the next 10 years or so, including the giant panda, tiger, and black rhino. A few of these animals survive in national parks and zoos, where they are protected.

Saving our wildlife

Extinct is forever

Animals become extinct (die out) for many reasons, such as a change in their habitat. For example, if the climate gets warmer, the animal may not survive this change.

Ancient animals

Crocodiles are ancient animals that were around when dinosaurs roamed Earth. Unlike the dinosaurs, crocodiles have survived. Other ancient animals still around include alligators and tortoises.

Saving our wildlife

We call an animal "endangered" when very few members of that species are alive. For example, the tiger is endangered because only a few thousand are left in the wild. An animal becomes extinct when the last one dies. Sadly, many thousands of different species, or kinds, of animal are endangered and hundreds become extinct every year.

Extreme habitats

Quick Quiz

Find the correct stickers to answer the questions below!

Which of these Arctic animals changes the color of its coat in winter?

seal

puffin

Arctic fox

Answer

Which of these desert animals licks its own eyeballs to stop them from drying out?

Answer

bat-eared fox   gecko   scorpion

Which of these urban animals is related to dogs and wolves?

racoon

fox

pigeon

Answer

Racoons

Racoons are found in North America, where they often visit yards and parks. These clever animals use their long fingers to open bags and boxes to get at any food inside.

Falcons eat other birds and small mammals, such as mice.

City pigeons

Pigeons are a common sight in many cities. They gather together in parks and other open spaces looking for food. They can be a nuisance because their droppings make a big mess.

Nesting falcons

Peregrine falcons build their nests on high buildings. From here, they have a good view of any prey moving around below.

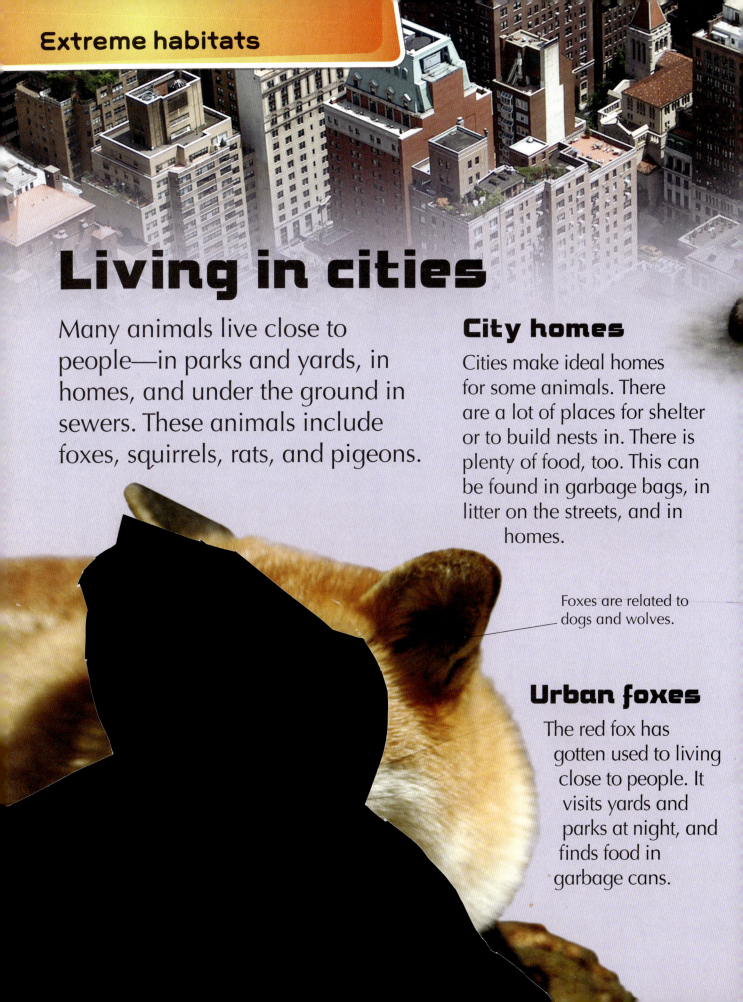

Extreme habitats

Living in cities

Many animals live close to people—in parks and yards, in homes, and under the ground in sewers. These animals include foxes, squirrels, rats, and pigeons.

City homes

Cities make ideal homes for some animals. There are a lot of places for shelter or to build nests in. There is plenty of food, too. This can be found in garbage bags, in litter on the streets, and in homes.

Foxes are related to dogs and wolves.

Urban foxes

The red fox has gotten used to living close to people. It visits yards and parks at night, and finds food in garbage cans.

Yaks

The yak is a large, shaggy animal that lives in the Himalaya Mountains in Asia. It has a thick coat to keep it warm in the cold mountain air.

Sure-footed

Mountain goats are found on the steepest cliffs, where they leap from ledge to ledge. They can do this because they have special hooves that grip the rock.

The name marmot comes from an old French word meaning "mountain mouse."

Whistling warning

Marmots are small animals that live in large groups on mountain slopes. Their warning call is a high-pitched whistle. When other marmots hear this whistle, they know danger is near and they run into their burrows.

Extreme habitats

Life on rocks and snow

Few animals can survive at the tops of mountains. There is very little to eat and the ground is covered in large, slippery boulders. Temperatures are low and snow lies on the ground all year round.

Did you know?

Mountain goats can leap almost 10 feet from one ledge to another. They can also turn around on ledges that are about an inch wide.

Mountain movers

Bighorn sheep move up mountains during the summer to feed on grasses on the high slopes. When winter comes, they move down again to escape the snow.

Bighorn sheep like open ground, where they can easily see any attackers.

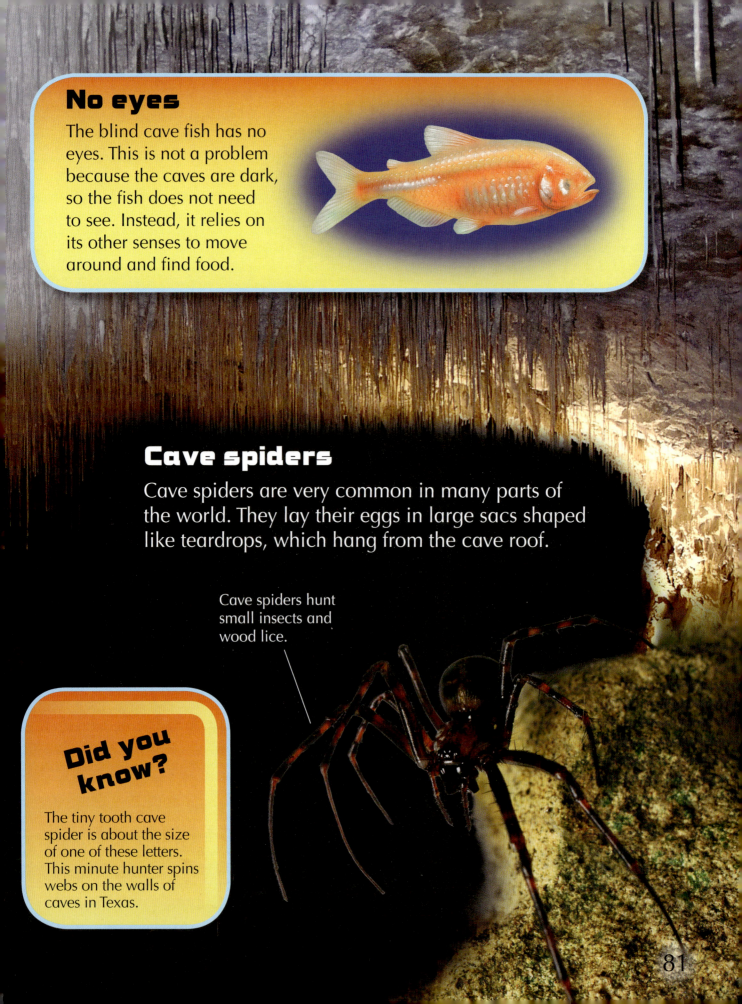

No eyes

The blind cave fish has no eyes. This is not a problem because the caves are dark, so the fish does not need to see. Instead, it relies on its other senses to move around and find food.

Cave spiders

Cave spiders are very common in many parts of the world. They lay their eggs in large sacs shaped like teardrops, which hang from the cave roof.

Cave spiders hunt small insects and wood lice.

Did you know?

The tiny tooth cave spider is about the size of one of these letters. This minute hunter spins webs on the walls of caves in Texas.

Extreme habitats

Living in caves

Many caves are cold and damp and often lie far below ground. Very little light can reach these places and the animals that live there have to cope with complete darkness.

Bat caves

Bats sleep, or roost, in caves during the day, hanging upside down with their claws gripping the cave walls. At night, they fly out to hunt.

Caves

Caves range in size from small hollows in a cliff to enormous cave networks that are hundreds of miles long.

Geckos

Geckos are small lizards. They run on the tips of their feet so that they do not get burned by the hot desert sand.

Geckos lick their eyeballs to stop them from drying out.

Did you know? Scientists have discovered remains of giant scorpions that were more than 5 feet long. These prehistoric monsters lived 330 million years ago.

The sting of some scorpions can kill people.

Scorpions

Some scorpions live in deserts. They are nocturnal, which means that they are active at night. They ambush prey and sting it with their tail stingers before eating it.

Extreme habitats

Locust swarms

Locusts form groups called swarms. They fly out of the desert and eat whole crops in neighboring regions.

Hot deserts

Most deserts are hot during the day, so animals creep under bushes or into holes to escape the sun. At night, the temperatures fall and it can be very cold.

The fox's large ears are very good at hearing prey running across the sand.

Nighttime hunter

Bat-eared foxes avoid the heat of the desert by sleeping in burrows during the day. They come out at night to hunt when it is cooler.

Multicolored beaks

Puffins catch small fish to eat and to feed to their young. They hold the fish in their colorful beaks and carry about 10 fish at a time.

Did you know?

Puffins are very good swimmers and can dive to depths of almost 200 feet to look for fish.

A new coat

The Arctic fox changes the color of its coat during the year to blend in with its surroundings. In winter, it has a white coat to hide in the snow. In summer, it turns brown to match the rocks and soil.

Extreme habitats

The Arctic

The Arctic is the region around the North Pole. This icy world has very long winters. In the middle of winter, the sun sets and does not rise again for several weeks.

Changing ice sheet

The Arctic is covered by a thick sheet of ice. During the summer, some of the ice melts and the sheet gets smaller. This means that land hunters, such as polar bears, have less area to hunt in, and they can struggle to find food.

Keeping warm

Seals have a thick layer of fat, called blubber, just beneath their skin. This keeps the seals warm in the icy Arctic seas.

Extreme habitats

Animals are incredibly adaptable. They can survive—and thrive—in some of the most hostile habitats on Earth, from burning deserts to rocky mountains and the snowy poles. Some have even adapted to live successfully alongside humans in our towns and cities.

Living in water

Quick Quiz

Find the correct stickers to answer the questions below!

Which of these animals has a mouth 5 feet wide?

Answer

whale shark   cuttlefish   sea turtle

Answer Which of these sea-dwelling creatures is a mammal?

giant clam   reef shark   beluga whale

Which of these animals is an amphibian?

Answer

newt   cichlid   angelfish

Freshwater fish

Many different kinds of fish are found in ponds and lakes, including this cichlid. Some fish feed on plants, while others hunt and eat other animals.

Plankton

Microscopic life

Pond water is full of tiny living things that are too small for us to see. These are called plankton and they include small plants, larvae (baby insects), and fish eggs.

Dragonfly larvae spend the first year of their lives in the water, hunting other animals.

Dragonfly larvae

Dragonflies lay their eggs in water. The young that hatch from the eggs are called larvae. When the larvae become adults, they leave the water and fly away.

Living in water

Lakes and ponds

The water in ponds and lakes is called still water because it hardly moves. Animals living there do not have to swim against a flow of water, as they do in streams and rivers.

Plant life

Plants, such as reeds, grow in the shallow water around the edges of lakes and ponds. Many animals like to hide among the plant stems and eat the leaves.

Newts

Newts belong to a group of animals called amphibians. They spend most of their time swimming in the water, but they also have legs so that they can walk across land.

This newt is brightly colored to warn other animals that it is poisonous.

Sea otters sometimes use rocks to smash open shellfish.

Sea otters

Sea otters swim through the kelp looking for sea urchins to eat. They even sleep in the kelp forests, wrapping themselves up in kelp leaves so they do not float away.

Eagle rays

Eagle rays have an excellent sense of smell. They like to sniff out mussels and other shellfish, which they crunch up using their strong teeth.

The large wings on an eagle ray can measure more than 6½ feet across.

Did you know? Giant kelp is one of the fastest growing plants in the world. When conditions are good, kelp can grow more than 1½ feet in a day!

Living in water

Kelp forests

Kelp is a type of giant seaweed that grows in underwater forests. These are found in shallow water near the ocean shore. The huge seaweed forests provide shelter for fish and other sea creatures.

Inside the forest

Giant kelp can grow to nearly 200 feet in length. It attaches itself to the ocean floor by roots called holdfasts. Thousands of fish swim between these massive blades of kelp, hiding from hunters, such as sharks.

Orange garibaldis

The bright orange color of the garibaldi fish is a warning to other fish in the forest to stay away. Garibaldis are very aggressive fish and will even attack human divers!

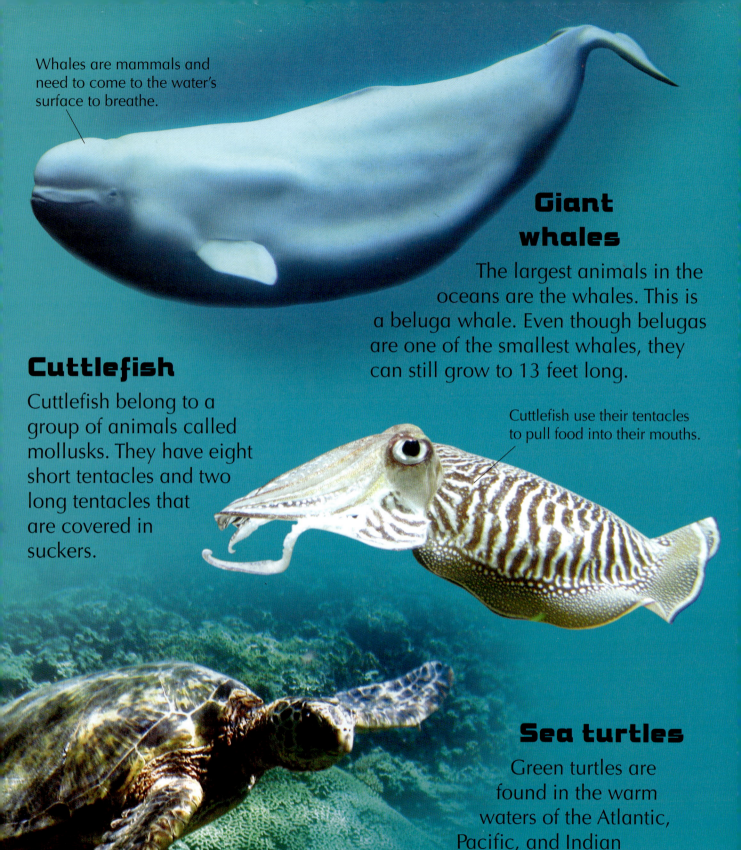

Whales are mammals and need to come to the water's surface to breathe.

Giant whales

The largest animals in the oceans are the whales. This is a beluga whale. Even though belugas are one of the smallest whales, they can still grow to 13 feet long.

Cuttlefish

Cuttlefish belong to a group of animals called mollusks. They have eight short tentacles and two long tentacles that are covered in suckers.

Cuttlefish use their tentacles to pull food into their mouths.

Sea turtles

Green turtles are found in the warm waters of the Atlantic, Pacific, and Indian oceans. They feed mainly on sea grasses and small plants called algae.

Living in water

Open ocean

The vast areas of open water between islands and continents are full of fish, whales, squid, and other animals. Most of these animals are found near the water's surface, where there is plenty of sunlight.

Huge but harmless

The whale shark is a huge fish. It swims near the ocean's surface, using its enormous mouth to strain tiny animals from the sea water.

A whale shark's mouth is 5 feet wide.

Did you know? Whale sharks are the largest fish swimming in the oceans. They often grow to more than 30 feet long.

Reef hunters

Reef sharks are among the largest hunters on the reef. Some sharks swim in groups, called packs, looking for small fish to eat.

Did you know? Scientists believe that some giant clams make their own sun screen. The clams' colors reflect light away from their bodies, protecting the clams from the strong sunlight.

Giant clam

Giant clams

Giant clams are bivalves, meaning they have two shells that are joined together. These huge shellfish can grow to more than 5 feet across.

Living in water

Coral reefs

Coral reefs are some of the richest habitats in the world. They are home to millions of different creatures, including hunting sharks and enormous shellfish.

Skeleton home

Coral reefs are made by tiny creatures called coral polyps. Some of the polyps have a hard outer covering called a skeleton. When the polyps die, the skeletons are left behind and gradually build up to form the reef.

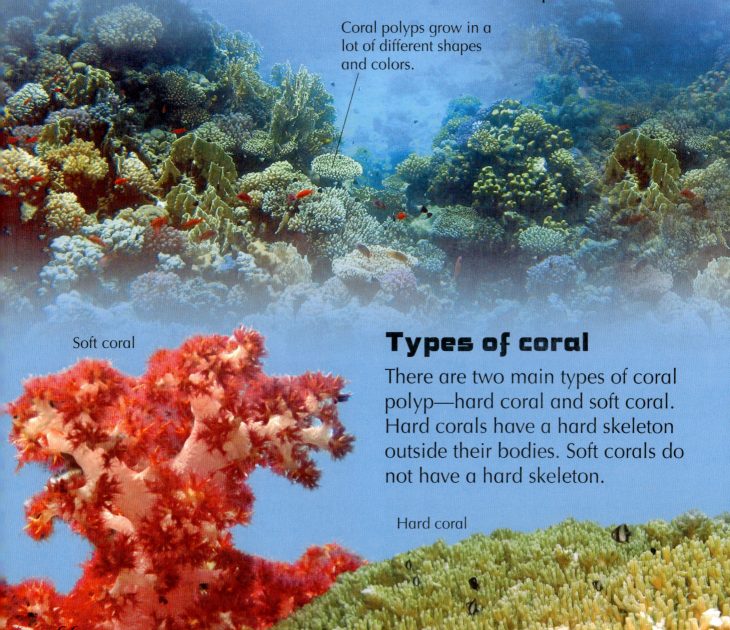

Coral polyps grow in a lot of different shapes and colors.

Soft coral

Hard coral

Types of coral

There are two main types of coral polyp—hard coral and soft coral. Hard corals have a hard skeleton outside their bodies. Soft corals do not have a hard skeleton.

Living in a group

Many types of fish swim together in large groups called schools. It is safer for fish to swim in schools because hunters can easily get confused by all the fish darting around.

A manta ray's wings can measure 23 feet across.

Flying underwater

A manta ray looks kind of like a huge plane underwater. Its fins extend from its body to create enormous wings. The ray swims by flapping these wings to "fly" through the water.

Living in water

How do fish swim?

Fish have powerful tails, which they move from side to side to push them through the water. They also have a number of fins on their bodies, which they use to guide them.

Did you know?

The sailfish is the fastest fish. It can swim at speeds of up to 68 miles per hour. This is faster than the fastest land mammal, the cheetah, can run.

Fast-swimming fish

The fastest fish in the seas are sailfish and tuna. Their bodies are streamlined, which means that they are thin and can slip through the water easily.

Tuna

Angelfish

Angelfish have a different body shape from tuna. Their bodies are squashed from side to side. This means they are not very fast swimmers, but they can twist and turn quickly.

Fish fins

A fish has a number of fins, each with a special job. The pectoral fins and the pelvic fins help with steering and stopping. The dorsal fin helps to keep the fish upright in the water.

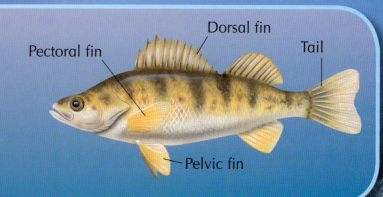

Pectoral fin, Dorsal fin, Tail, Pelvic fin

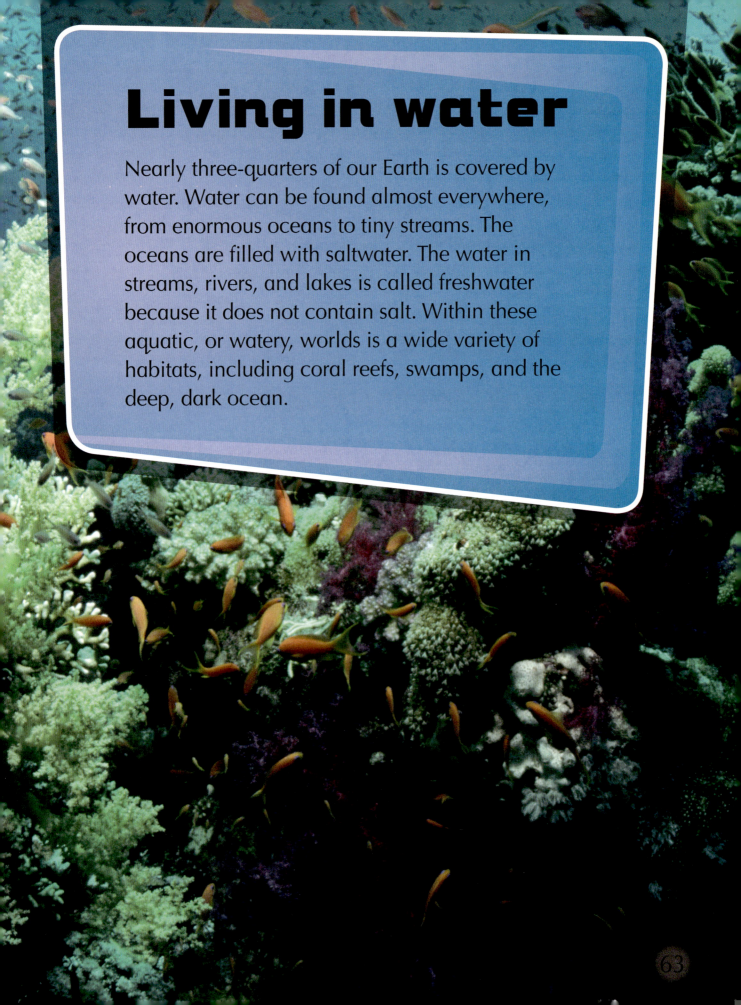

Living in water

Nearly three-quarters of our Earth is covered by water. Water can be found almost everywhere, from enormous oceans to tiny streams. The oceans are filled with saltwater. The water in streams, rivers, and lakes is called freshwater because it does not contain salt. Within these aquatic, or watery, worlds is a wide variety of habitats, including coral reefs, swamps, and the deep, dark ocean.

Forests and grasslands

Quick Quiz

Find the correct stickers to answer the questions below!

Which of these rain-forest animals can change color?

katydid

scarlet macaw

chameleon

Answer

Which of these animals is a type of pig?

Answer

wild boar

white-tailed deer

spotted hyena

Which of these animals is a carnivore?

rabbit

red fox

llama

Answer

Red fox

The red fox is a carnivore, or meat eater. It is usually active at night, when it hunts for small mammals, such as rabbits. It also feeds on berries.

Did you know?

A single pair of rabbits will have as many as 40 babies in a year.

Pack animals

Llamas are found on the grassy slopes of the Andes Mountains in South America. These plant eaters live in groups called herds and are used by local people to carry heavy loads.

Llamas are related to camels.

Forests and grasslands

Cool grasslands

Grasslands found in the cooler parts of the world are called temperate grasslands. These regions are warm in the summer and may be covered in snow in the winter.

Digging hunter

The badger uses its long, sharp claws to dig small animals, such as ground squirrels and mice, out of the ground.

Rabbits thump the ground with their back legs to warn other rabbits of danger.

Good listener

The rabbit has long ears, which give it a good sense of hearing. It uses these to listen for any hunters that may be nearby.

The great migration

Each year, huge herds of zebras and wildebeest make long journeys in search of fresh grass to eat. This is called a migration. The migration is dangerous because the animals have to cope with fast-flowing rivers and hunters, such as crocodiles.

Meerkats keep a sharp eye out for hunters, such as snakes or jackals.

On guard

Meerkats live in large groups in burrows under the grasslands of southern Africa. Each member of the group has a job to do. Some are babysitters or teachers, while others are guards or hunters.

Forests and grasslands

Warm grasslands

Grasslands are large areas of flat ground covered by grasses. Warm grasslands, or savannahs, are found in Africa, South America, and Australia. During the dry months the grasses turn yellow. However, once the rains fall, the grasslands turn green.

Did you know?

The hyena is often called the laughing hyena because of its noisy cackle or laughlike call.

A sea of grass

Some of the grasses on the savannah are taller than people. There are only a few trees, such as acacias and baobabs. Most of the young trees are eaten before they can grow very tall.

Bone-crushing hyenas

Spotted hyenas are hunters that live on the grasslands of Africa. They have strong jaws and huge teeth that can crush the bones of their prey as if they were twigs.

Sharp leaves

Conifer trees have leaves shaped like needles. These leaves are very sharp, and they are not very good for animals to eat.

Laying eggs

The wood wasp, or horntail, lays its eggs in the bark of conifer trees. The female has a long, pointed tube at the end of her body, which she digs into the bark to lay her eggs.

Egg-laying tube

Team birds

The northern forests are home to many birds. This blue jay lives in forests in North America. Blue jays will work together and attack other animals that get too close to their nests.

Forest hunters

The lynx is one of the hunting animals that live in the northern forests. It climbs up a tree and waits for an animal to pass close by before leaping down and attacking.

Forests and grasslands

Northern forests

Did you know?
As deer's antlers grow, they become covered in a furry skin called velvet.

A band of evergreen forests stretches across the top of North America, Europe, and Asia. The trees that grow here are called conifers. Winters are long and cold, and there are fewer animals than in warmer forests because there is little food to eat.

Grazing deer

Large deer live in the northern coniferous forests, feeding off grass, twigs, and bark. Some deer grow huge antlers on top of their heads. At the end of each year, these antlers drop off and new ones start to grow.

Male white-tailed deer use their antlers to fight each other in fall. This is called rutting.

Forest birds

Temperate forests are home to many birds. The birds eat the seeds and fruit that grow on the trees, as well as insects living there. The birds also build nests in the branches.

Wrens hunt for insects in holes and cracks on trees.

Wild boar

Wild boar are large pigs that live in forests. They eat roots, fruit, and berries that lie on the forest floor. Male boars have curved teeth called tusks, which stick out of their mouths.

Did you know?

The largest tree, the Sequoia, can grow to more than 330 feet tall and live for 2,000 years.

Forests and grasslands

Mixed forests

Temperate forests are found in cool parts of the world. They are a mixture of trees that lose their leaves in winter (deciduous trees) and trees that keep their leaves during the cold months (evergreen trees).

Losing leaves

Deciduous trees lose their leaves because they do not get enough water in the winter. The water in the ground freezes, making it impossible for trees to collect it through their roots. The leaves turn brown and fall off.

Millipedes eat the leaves that fall off the trees.

Living on the floor

The forest floor is covered in plants and fallen leaves. These make it an ideal home for many small animals, such as millipedes.

This katydid is colored green so that it can hide among the leaves.

Insects in the canopy

Many different kinds of insect are found in the canopy, where they eat leaves. These insects may be eaten by larger animals, such as birds or lizards.

Tough beak

The scarlet macaw has a powerful hooked beak. It uses this to crack open nuts and as an extra claw to climb up the trunks of trees.

Chameleons catch insects to eat using their very long tongues.

Clever camouflage

Chameleons can change the color of their skin so that they blend in with the leaves of the trees. This is called camouflage and it makes chameleons difficult to see.

Forests and grasslands

Life in the canopy

Most of the rain-forest animals live high in the trees. This is called the canopy. They have learned how to move from tree to tree and where to find food and water. Some animals never come down to the ground.

Orange ape
Orangutans have long arms and legs. Their fingers are hooked to help them grip branches as they climb through the trees looking for fruit.

Did you know?
Although most chameleons eat insects, a few species are big enough to catch and eat birds.

Colorful beak
The toucan eats fruit. It uses its long beak to reach fruit that grows at the ends of small branches.

Forests and grasslands

The place where an animal lives is called its habitat. A habitat is made up of a community, or group, of plants and animals. Forests and grasslands, from African savannas to northern evergreen forests, are important habitats for land-dwelling animals.

Living in the air

Quick Quiz

Find the correct stickers to answer the questions below!

Which of these creatures is a mammal?

Answer

hummingbird   bat   butterfly

Which of these birds builds its nest out of small balls of mud or clay?

Answer

swallow   owl   cuckoo

Which of these birds can have wings nearly 6½ feet across?

Answer

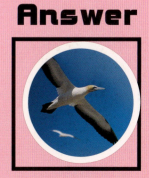

blue tit   weaver bird   gannet

Buzzing bees

The honeybee has two pairs of very thin wings. It beats these wings so quickly that they make a buzzing sound. A bee can fly at 20 miles per hour.

Did you know?

Most insects do not use their mouths to make sounds. Instead, they rub their wings or legs together to make a noise.

Colorful butterflies

Butterfly wings are covered in tiny scales. These scales can be a wide variety of colors.

Ladybug wings

The ladybug has a pair of tough red and black wings. These cover a second pair of wings, which are very delicate. The ladybug uses the second pair for flying.

Living in the air

Flying insects

Most insects have two pairs of wings, which they use to fly. Insect wings vary in shape, from the thin wings of bees to the large, colorful wings of butterflies.

Insect hunters

Dragonflies have two pairs of long, see-through wings. These powerful insects are excellent fliers, and can catch smaller insects in midair.

Hard to catch

Houseflies have only one pair of wings, but they are still among the fastest insects. They use their speed to escape attackers.

Dragonflies have large eyes for finding prey.

Fruit bats

Fruit bats live in the forests of Africa, Australia, and Asia. Some fruit bats have extra-long tongues, which they use to suck nectar out of flowers.

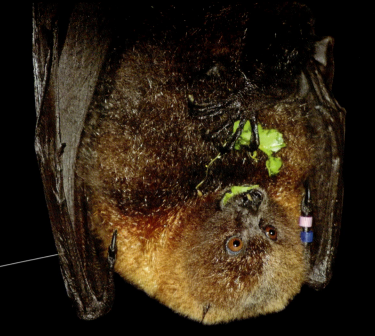

Fruit bats are sometimes called flying foxes.

Bats in flight

A bat has powerful chest muscles, which it uses to flap its wings. It steers by moving the bones in its fingers and legs to change the wing's shape.

The bat wing

The bones in a bat's fingers are extra-long and are covered by a thin layer of skin which forms the wing. A thumb sticks out from the top of the wing and ends in a claw.

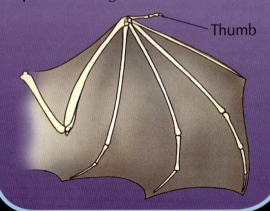

Thumb

Fruit bat camp

Fruit bats gather in large groups high in the branches of rainforest trees. These groups are called camps.

Living in the air

Bats

Bats are the only mammals that can fly. Instead of front legs, they have wings. They do not walk with their back legs, but use them to hang upside down.

Roosting bats

Most bats are nocturnal, which means that they are active at night. They sleep during the day, hanging by their feet from the walls of caves, buildings, and trees. This is called roosting.

Did you know?

Some fruit bats have wings that measure almost 6½ feet from tip to tip.

There are nearly 1,000 species of bat.

Baby birds

Newly hatched chicks are weak and parents must give them all the food they need. Sometimes parents will swallow the food and then bring it back up for the chicks to eat.

Did you know?

Ostriches lay the largest birds' eggs. Each egg is about 7 inches long and weighs 2½ pounds.

Leaving the nest

As the chicks grow, the parents bring back more and more food. When the chicks are strong enough, they will try a few short practice flights. Then they will leave the nest for good.

This eagle chick is now ready to leave its nest.

Living in the air

Growing birds

All birds lay eggs. The parent birds take care of the eggs to make sure the chicks, or baby birds, hatch. The chicks are then fed until they are big enough to leave the nest.

Keeping warm

Birds' eggs must be kept warm for the chicks to hatch. The parents do this by sitting on top of the eggs. This is called incubation.

Nest imposters

Cuckoos do not build nests. Instead, they lay their eggs in the nests of other birds, who then take care of the baby cuckoos. Baby cuckoos are bigger than the other chicks in the nest, so they get most of the food.

Weaving a nest

Weaver birds build their nests by weaving thin twigs and reeds together. Woven nests usually have narrow entrances to stop egg-eating animals from getting inside.

Massive platforms

Some birds, such as storks and eagles, build large platform nests out of sticks and twigs. The largest platforms can measure more than 6½ feet across and 20 feet deep.

A spectacled weaver bird stands at the narrow entrance to its nest.

Small birds, such as blue tits, are safe from hunters in a birdhouse.

Birdhouse

A good way to attract birds into the garden is to put up a birdhouse. Birds then build their nest inside.

Living in the air

Building nests

Most birds build nests in which they lay their eggs. Different birds build different shapes of nest, which range from simple cup shapes to enormous platforms.

This paradise flycatcher has made its nest from twigs, leaves, and moss.

Building materials

Nests are made from a variety of materials, such as twigs, leaves, moss, wool, and feathers. Some birds even use human garbage to build their nests.

Swallow nests

Swallows build their nests out of small balls of mud and clay. Each nest can contain 1,500 balls of clay.

Did you know?

The vervain hummingbird builds the smallest bird's nest, which is about the size of half a walnut shell.

Silent fliers

Some owls do not make a sound when they fly. They have soft feathers along the fronts of their wings, which quiet the sound of the air as it passes over the wings.

Fast flight

Swallows have short wings that let them fly quickly and dart to catch flying insects. If they need to dive, they pull their wings into their bodies and drop like a stone.

Some hummingbirds flap their wings 1,200 times a minute.

Hovering hummingbirds

Hummingbirds are small birds that can hover. They stay in one place by beating their wings backward and forward very quickly. This allows them to hover in front of a flower, so that they can reach in and drink nectar.

Living in the air

Birds' wings

Birds have wings instead of arms. They fly by extending and flapping their wings. The wings are made from a number of bones with feathers attached to them. They can be long and broad, or short and narrow.

Gliding through air

Gliding birds, such as gannets, use currents of moving air to fly. These birds have very large wings that catch the currents and carry the birds into the air.

Some gannets have wings that measure nearly 6½ feet across.

Robin Pheasant Swallow

Eagle Gull

Wing shapes

Birds that fly by gliding and soaring, such as eagles and gulls, have large wings with long feathers. Birds that fly short distances and need to dart quickly, such as robins, pheasants, and swallows, have short wings that they flap quickly.

40

Living in the air

Many animals have learned how to fly through the air. These include birds, insects, and bats. They fly using wings made from feathers or flaps of skin, which they flap to lift them off the ground. Flying lets these animals hunt for food in the air and helps them to escape from predators.

Types of animals

Quick Quiz

Find the correct stickers to answer the questions below!

Which of these creatures has stinging tentacles?

Answer

  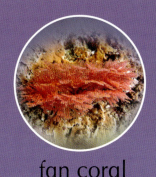 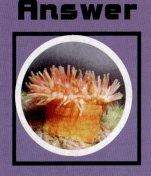

anemone   sponge   fan coral

Answer   Which of these creatures is not an arachnid?

black widow spider   scorpion   cockroach

Which of these birds cannot fly?

Answer

swan   ostrich   heron

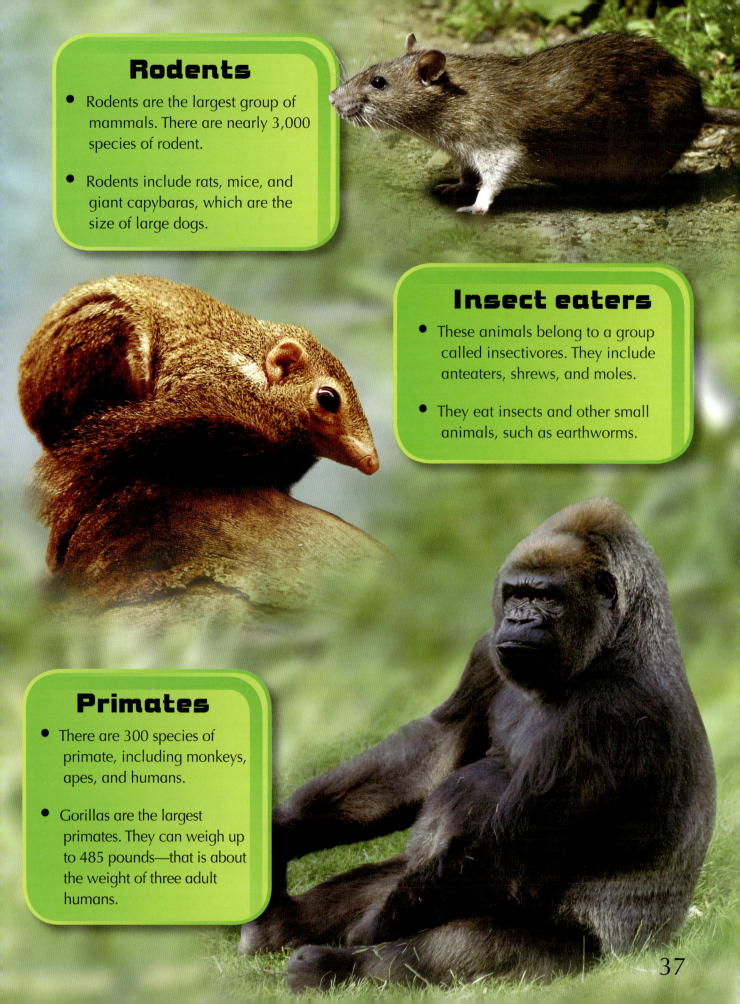

Rodents

- Rodents are the largest group of mammals. There are nearly 3,000 species of rodent.
- Rodents include rats, mice, and giant capybaras, which are the size of large dogs.

Insect eaters

- These animals belong to a group called insectivores. They include anteaters, shrews, and moles.
- They eat insects and other small animals, such as earthworms.

Primates

- There are 300 species of primate, including monkeys, apes, and humans.
- Gorillas are the largest primates. They can weigh up to 485 pounds—that is about the weight of three adult humans.

Types of animals

Mammals

Mammals are animals whose bodies are covered in fur. Most of them give birth to live young instead of laying eggs. Female mammals then make milk to feed their young.

Platypus

- The platypus is unusual because it is a mammal that lays eggs.

- It has a ducklike beak and webbed feet to help it swim. It also has small poisonous spurs on its back legs to defend itself with.

Pouch

Kangaroos

- Kangaroos belong to a group of mammals called marsupials. Female marsupials have pouches to carry their young around in.

- There are more than 300 kinds of marsupial, including koalas and wombats.

Pelicans

- Pelicans have a long beak with a pouch underneath it. They use these pouches to scoop fish out of the water.

- Brown pelicans catch fish by diving from the air into a group of fish underwater.

Gulls

- There are 40 species, or kinds, of these large, web-footed seabirds.

- They hunt for food on beaches, eating worms, shellfish, and even human garbage. Larger gulls will steal and eat eggs and the young of other birds.

Gulls use their large wings to glide through the air.

Swans use their long necks to reach down to the riverbed to eat pondweed.

Aquatic birds

- Birds in this group include ducks, geese, and swans. All of these birds have webbed feet and they can swim and float on water.

- Their feathers are covered in an oil that stops them from absorbing water. Without this oil, the birds would sink.

Types of animals

Birds

Birds are animals that lay eggs and whose bodies are covered in feathers. All birds have two wings—even the ones that cannot fly.

Egret

Herons

- Herons belong to a group of birds that includes egrets.
- They are wading birds and have long legs so that they can stand in water looking for fish.

If attacked, an ostrich can kick its long legs to defend itself.

Flightless birds

- There are several kinds of birds that do not fly. They include penguins and emus.
- Ostriches are the world's largest birds. They have very long legs and can run up to 40 miles per hour.

Tortoises

- Like turtles, tortoises have large shells that protect their bodies.

- Tortoises have short legs, which they use to walk slowly over the ground, usually at speeds of just one-tenth of a mile per hour.

Crocodiles

- Crocodiles are hunters that eat birds, mammals, and fish.

- Crocodiles lay more than 100 eggs at a time. They build nests that are specially designed to keep the eggs warm.

Tuataras

- These reptiles are only found in New Zealand. They are related to both snakes and lizards.

- A tuatara has a special third eye on top of its head. Some scientists think the tuatara uses this to control its body heat.

Types of animals

Reptiles

Reptiles are animals that have scaly skin. Some kinds of reptile spend a lot of time in water, but they all lay their eggs on land.

Turtles

- Turtles can pull their heads and legs inside their hard shells for protection from attackers.

- Turtles are found in lakes and rivers, and in warm seas. Some sea turtles can swim huge distances, covering 310 miles in just 10 days.

Crocodiles tuck their legs into their sides when they swim through the water.

Alligators

- These reptiles have long bodies with short legs and long tails, which they flick to push them through the water. They eat fish, small mammals, and birds.

- Alligators have wide snouts, while crocodiles usually have narrow snouts.

Toads

- There are more than 300 species, or kinds, of toad. They eat insects and other small animals, which they catch with their tongues.

- Some kinds of toad make a poison that can paralyze and even kill an attacker.

Salamanders

- Salamanders are closely related to newts. They live in rivers, lakes, and woodlands in cool parts of the world.

- The largest salamander is the giant salamander. It can grow to a length of 5 feet.

Frogs

- Frogs have long legs that are ideal for leaping, as well as webbed feet that are good for swimming.

- They have smooth skin and jump around, while toads have bumpy skin and hop.

Types of animals

Amphibians

Amphibians are animals that spend their adult lives on land, but they return to the water to lay their eggs. Their young grow up in the water, but they move onto land when they are adults.

Poison arrow frogs

- These frogs are small, but they are very poisonous. Their bright colors warn other animals to stay away.

- They live in the forests of South America, hunting insects and other small creatures.

Newts

- Newts have long, thin bodies with long tails that are flattened from top to bottom.

- If a newt loses a leg or even an eye, it can grow back the missing body part. This is called regeneration.

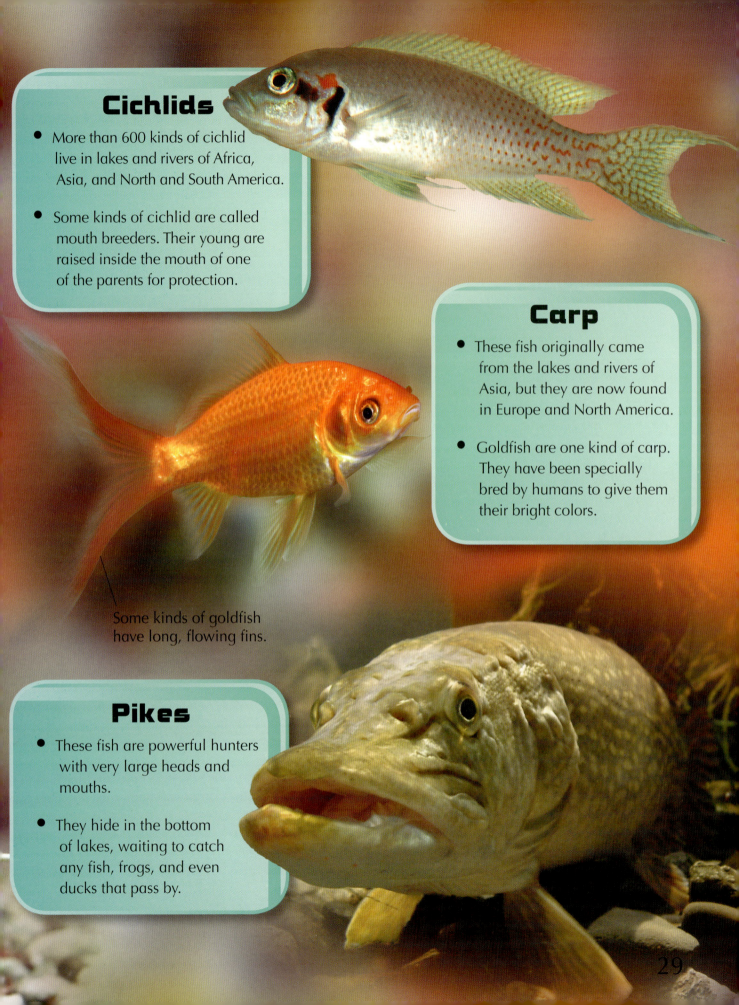

Cichlids

- More than 600 kinds of cichlid live in lakes and rivers of Africa, Asia, and North and South America.

- Some kinds of cichlid are called mouth breeders. Their young are raised inside the mouth of one of the parents for protection.

Carp

- These fish originally came from the lakes and rivers of Asia, but they are now found in Europe and North America.

- Goldfish are one kind of carp. They have been specially bred by humans to give them their bright colors.

Some kinds of goldfish have long, flowing fins.

Pikes

- These fish are powerful hunters with very large heads and mouths.

- They hide in the bottom of lakes, waiting to catch any fish, frogs, and even ducks that pass by.

Types of animals

Freshwater fish

Freshwater fish live in rivers, streams, and lakes. There are very few fish that can live in both freshwater and saltwater.

Piranhas

- Piranhas live in the lakes and rivers of South America and grow to 24 inches long.

- They hunt in packs and attack other animals, using their razor-sharp teeth to bite out lumps of meat.

The teeth in a piranha's mouth slice together like a pair of scissors.

Catfish

- Catfish have feelers that stick out from around their mouths. These feelers look like cats' whiskers and are called barbels.

- Catfish use these barbels to find food that is hidden in the mud of riverbeds.

Eels

- There are about 400 different species, or kinds, of eel. These fish have long, snakelike bodies.

- Some eels, such as this moray eel, hide in holes in warm, shallow water. They leap out and grab prey as it passes by.

Sea dragons have long fins and flaps on their bodies to make them look like pieces of seaweed.

Sea dragons

- Sea dragons use their long fins to paddle slowly through the water as they look for small plants and animals to eat.

- Sea dragons can grow to 18 inches in length.

Angelfish

- Angelfish live on coral reefs in the Indian, Atlantic, and Pacific oceans.

- These fish have flat bodies with long fins and small mouths. The patterns on their bodies change as the fish get older.

Types of animals

Ocean fish

Fish are vertebrates, meaning they have backbones. They live in water and breathe using gills.

Sharks

- Most sharks are hunters and chase prey, such as fish, squid, and crabs. A few sharks are not hunters. Instead, they eat tiny plants and animals, called plankton.

- Instead of bone, sharks have a skeleton made from a bendy substance called cartilage.

Gills

Rays

- Rays have flat bodies and they swim by flapping their sides—just like the wings of birds—to "fly" through the water.

- Some rays have poisonous spines on their tails, which they flick up when they are threatened.

Sunstars

- Sunstars are a kind of starfish. They have between 8 and 16 arms and can measure 14 inches across.

- They crawl over the ocean floor hunting for shellfish and other starfish to eat.

Sea urchins

- Sea urchins are ball-shaped animals that are covered in spines.

- They hide in cracks between rocks. Their spines make it difficult for hunters to catch them and pull them out.

Sand dollars

- Sand dollars are a kind of urchin, with a flat body shaped like a coin.

- They live on beaches and burrow into the sand when the tide goes out.

25

Types of animals

Starfish, urchins, and cucumbers

These creatures belong to the group of animals called echinoderms. They are found in the ocean, where they live on the seashore, ocean floor, and coral reefs. Echinoderms do not have eyes, brains, or hearts.

Sea cucumbers

- These sluglike creatures have leathery or spiky skin and grow to a length of 6½ feet.

- Some kinds of sea cucumber throw out sticky threads when attacked in order to confuse any hunters.

Starfish can regrow any arms that they lose.

Starfish

- There are more than 1,800 different kinds of starfish. They usually have five arms that are attached to a central body.

- Some kinds of starfish have as many as 50 arms.

Limpets

- These mollusks are covered with cone-shaped shells and live on rocks along the ocean shore.

- Limpets move slowly over the rocks, eating tiny plants called algae. When the tide goes out, limpets pull their shells down tight and stick to the rocks.

Sea slugs

- Many sea slugs are brightly colored. This warns other animals that they are poisonous.

- Sea slugs feed on other animals, including sponges and, sometimes, other sea slugs.

A snail moves along by stretching out its large foot.

Snails

- Snails have coil-shaped shells and are found living on land as well as rivers, lakes, and the ocean.

- When threatened, a snail will retreat into its shell and close a plate, called an operculum, over the opening.

Types of animals

Mollusks

Mollusks are invertebrates, which means they do not have backbones. They either have shells around the outside of their bodies or the remains of shells inside their bodies.

Cuttlefish can change color to hide from hunters.

Cuttlefish

- Cuttlefish are related to octopuses and squid. They have shells inside their bodies.

- Cuttlefish have eight short tentacles and two long ones, which they use to catch prey. They swim backward by forcing water out of their bodies in powerful jets.

Clams

- Clams are bivalves. This means that they have two shells that are hinged, so that they can open and close.

- Giant clams can be more than 3 feet long and weigh more than 440 pounds.

Hunting spiders

- These spiders do not build webs. Instead, they hunt down prey or ambush unsuspecting animals.
- Hunting spiders include wolf spiders, tarantulas, and huntsman spiders.

Some female ticks can suck up to 100 times their body weight in blood.

Ticks and mites

- Ticks and mites are parasites that live on and feed off other animals. They use their jaws to suck the other animals' blood.
- Some ticks and mites will rest on top of long blades of grass, waiting to jump onto passing animals.

Scorpions

- A scorpion has four pairs of legs. The front pair ends in pincers.
- The scorpion's tail curves over its body and ends in a stinger that is used to paralyze prey.

Types of animals

Arachnids

This group of animals includes spiders, scorpions, mites, and ticks. Arachnids have eight legs and, unlike insects, they only have two body parts: a head-thorax and a separate abdomen.

Web-weaving spiders

- Many kinds of spider produce thin threads of silk. Some weave the silk into sticky webs, which they use to trap prey.

- Some spiders eat their webs at the end of each day when the stickiness has worn off. They then build fresh webs.

Orb-weaving spiders wrap their prey up in spider silk before feeding.

The black widow spider has one of the most powerful poisons in the world.

Poisonous spiders

- These spiders use poison to harm or kill other animals. The bite of about 200 kinds of spider can cause pain to a human or even death.

- A spider can choose whether or not to inject poison when it bites.

Millipedes

- Unlike centipedes, millipedes are not hunters. Instead, they eat plants.

- To protect themselves, millipedes roll up into tight coils. Some kinds of millipede give off a foul-smelling liquid, which scares off any hunters.

Giant millipedes

- Giant millipedes can grow to a length of nearly 16 inches and are as thick as your thumb.

- The largest millipedes have more than 100 segments to their bodies.

Pill millipedes

- Pill millipedes are much shorter than other millipedes and are often mistaken for wood lice.

- When threatened, they can roll up into balls to protect themselves.

Some kinds of millipede can jump an inch when they are attacked.

Types of animals

Centipedes and millipedes

Centipedes and millipedes have long bodies that are split into many segments, or sections. Centipedes have one pair of legs on each segment. Millipedes have two pairs of legs per segment.

Centipedes

- There are more than 5,000 different kinds of centipede. They usually live in woodlands, among fallen leaves, except for house centipedes, which can spend their entire lives inside buildings.

- All centipedes are poisonous and use their poison to kill their prey.

House centipedes have very long legs that let them run quickly.

Giant centipedes

- These are the largest kind of centipede. Some can grow to a foot long.

- They are hunting centipedes. They come out at night and search for their prey which can include vertebrate animals, such as mice.

Wood lice

- These crustaceans live on land, usually in dark and damp places, where they eat rotting wood.
- Some wood lice roll up into tight balls for protection.

Water flea

- Water fleas, such as daphnia, are found in the fresh water of lakes and rivers, but a few live in the ocean.
- Most water fleas are usually too small to see with the naked eye. However, some are as large as half an inch long.

Daphnia wave their antennae, or feelers, to move through the water.

Lobsters

- Lobsters have five pairs of legs. One or more of these pairs ends in pincers called chelae.
- Lobsters can either walk along the ocean floor or swim through the water by flicking their long tails.

Types of animals

Crustaceans

A crustacean has a body that is covered with a tough shell called an external skeleton. Most crustaceans live in the water, but a few can survive on land.

Crabs

- Crabs live in the ocean, on land, and in rivers. Their bodies are protected by thick shells called carapaces.

- The front legs on crabs have developed into large pinching claws which the crabs use to hold objects and prey.

Shrimp

- There are about 2,000 kinds of shrimp. They have a long, thin body covered in a see-through shell.

- All shrimp swim backwards by twitching their bodies and tails.

Cockroaches

- Cockroaches are some of the oldest insects on Earth. They have been around for 320 million years.

- Cockroaches have long, flattened bodies that are covered in tough external, or outer, skeletons.

Eye

Dragonflies

- Dragonflies have two pairs of wings that are usually see-through and many have long, thin abdomens.

- Dragonflies have huge eyes which let them see completely around their bodies.

Dragonflies keep their wings open when resting.

Abdomen   Thorax   Head

Ants

- An ant has a large head and a long, oval-shaped abdomen that is joined to the thorax by a thin waist.

- Most kinds of ant live together in huge groups, called colonies.

15

Types of animals

Insects

Insects belong to a very large group of creatures called arthropods. Adult insects have three body parts: a head, a middle section called the thorax, and a tail section called the abdomen. They all have six legs.

Fleas

- Fleas are tiny insects that are parasites. This means that they live on, and feed off, other animals.

- Fleas have powerful back legs and can jump 150 times their body length.

Butterflies

- There are 17,500 different species, or kinds, of butterfly.

- Butterflies have two pairs of wings. Each pair is joined together by tiny hooks, so that they flap at the same time.

This swallowtail butterfly has a fork-shaped tail, just like the swallow bird.

Roundworms

- Roundworms live on land and in the water, as well as inside other animals.

- Most roundworms are too small to see with the naked eye. However, the largest are 26 feet long and live in whales.

Fan worms wave their tentacles in the water to trap any passing food.

Fan worms

- These are segmented worms that are found on the ocean floor. They live inside tubes that they dig in the mud.

- When fan worms want to eat, they stretch their tentacles out of the ends of their tubes.

Lugworms

- Lugworms live in the mud on beaches and around the mouths of rivers. They dig burrows into the mud.

- They suck water into these burrows and filter out food particles to eat.

Types of animals

Worms

Worms are animals without backbones. Many live in water, while others live underground. Some worms live inside the bodies of animals and are called parasites.

Earthworms

- Earthworms are a kind of segmented worm. Their bodies are split into sections called segments.

- Earthworms feed on dead and rotting leaves, which they pull into the tunnels they dig in the soil.

Tapeworms use these sharp hooks to dig into the guts of animals.

Tapeworms

- Tapeworms are parasites that live in the guts of other animals. They feed off the other animals' food.

- Some tapeworms can grow to 50 feet in length.

Jellyfish

- Jellyfish have bell-shaped bodies at the top with a lot of stinging tentacles hanging below.

- They eat small animals and plants that they catch in their tentacles.

Fan corals

- Fan corals are made up of millions of tiny creatures called polyps. Polyps look a little like tiny anemones.

- Fan corals are found in warm oceans and can grow to nearly 10 feet in size.

Staghorn coral gets its name because it looks like the antlers of a stag.

Hard corals

- Hard corals have tough skeletons that are left behind after the animals die. These skeletons build up over many years to form coral reefs.

- Staghorn corals can grow up to 8 inches every year.

Types of animals

Sponges, anemones, and jellyfish

Anemones
- Anemones have rings of arms, called tentacles, around their mouths.
- These tentacles can sting other animals. Anemones use their stinging tentacles to catch their food and pull it into their mouths.

Sponges, anemones, and jellyfish are invertebrates, or animals without backbones. They live in water and have a tube-shaped body that is open at one end.

Mouth

Tentacles

These are tube sponges. They can be 3 feet long.

Sponges
- Sponges always remain anchored to the ocean floor.
- They feed by drawing water through holes in their bodies and filtering out tiny plants and animals.

Wing

Birds have beaks, large breast bones, and wings.

Breast bone

Most mammals, such as cats, have four legs.

What's inside?

Scientists study the insides of animals' bodies to see what animal group they belong to. For example, different types of animals have different shaped skeletons.

Reptiles, such as crocodiles, have long skulls.

Outer appearance

Sometimes you can tell what group an animal belongs to just by looking at it. For instance, birds have bodies that are covered in feathers, mammals usually have bodies covered in hair, and reptiles have scales.

A shark is a fish. It has fins instead of legs, uses gills instead of lungs, and is covered in scales.

Fin

Gills

Types of animals

Grouping animals

All animals belong to a group called the animal kingdom. This is divided into two groups, which are divided again and again into ever-smaller groups. An individual animal, such as the polar bear, is known as a species.

Polar bears belong to a group of animals called mammals.

Backbones

Animals are divided into two groups: those without backbones, called invertebrates, and those with backbones—vertebrates. These are split again. For example, vertebrates divide into fish, amphibians, reptiles, birds, and mammals.

What is a polar bear?

- It belongs to the animal kingdom.
- It is a vertebrate (has a backbone).
- It is a mammal (mothers make milk).
- It is a bear (a kind of mammal).
- It is a polar bear (its common name).

Types of animals

There are more than one-and-a-half million different types, or species, of animals in the world—and there are millions more still waiting to be discovered. Scientists group animals together according to their features. So, for example, animals with six legs belong to a group called insects. By studying an animal's features, we can figure out what group it belongs to.

Contents

Types of animals	6
Living in the air	39
Forests and grasslands	51
Living in water	63
Extreme habitats	75
Saving our wildlife	87
Index	94

Author: Sally Morgan
Consultant: Mandy Holloway

First published by Parragon in 2008
Parragon
Queen Street House
4 Queen Street
Bath BA1 1HE, UK

Copyright © Parragon Books Ltd 2008

©2008 Discovery Communications, LLC. Discovery Kids, DiscoveryFacts and related logos and indicia are trademarks of Discovery Communications, LLC, used under license. All rights reserved. discoverykids.com

All rights reserved. No part of this publication may be reproduced, stored in a retrieval system or transmitted, in any form or by any means, electronic, mechanical, photocopying, recording or otherwise, without the prior permission of the copyright holder.

ISBN 978-1-4075-4456-4
Printed in China

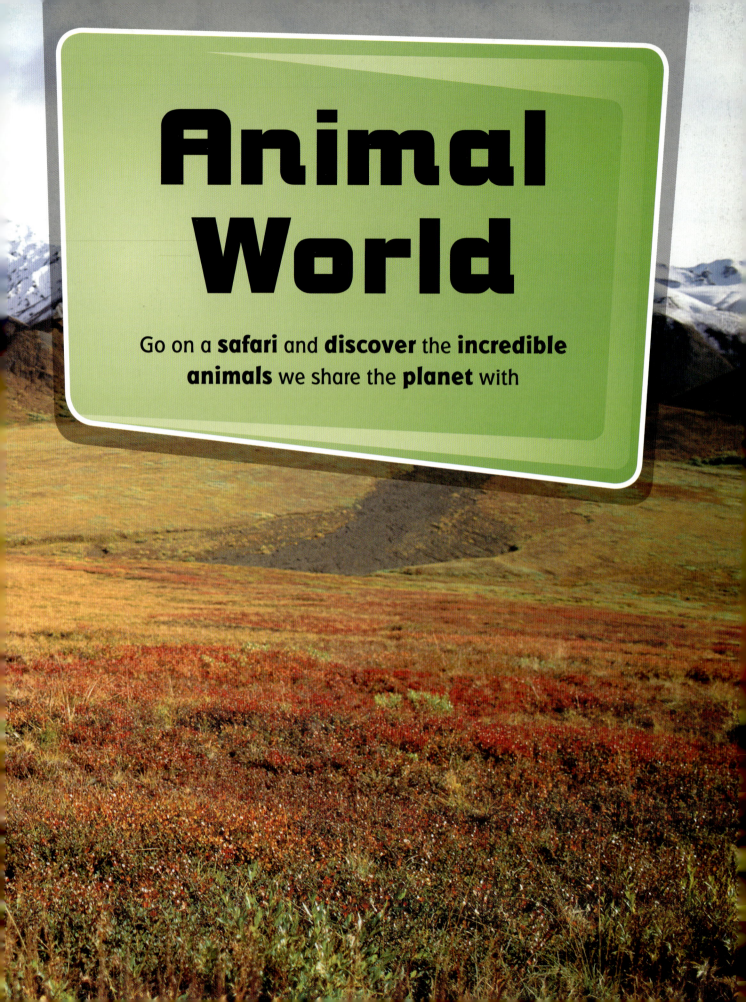

Animal World

Go on a **safari** and **discover** the **incredible animals** we share the **planet** with